100
REASONS
WHY I HATE
Poverty

COURAGE IGENE

100 Reasons Why I Hate Poverty

Paperback ISBN 978-0-9883707-5-3
Library of Congress Control Number 2012952122

Published by
GodKulture Publishing
Chicago, Illinois

Phone: 402-419-1072
Email: publishing@Godkulture.org
www.Godkulturepublishing.com

Printed in the United States of America

ACKNOWLEDGMENT

Special Thanks To My Special Partners

Who Invested

Their Prayers and Finances

To Make This Book Possible!

You Are Truly Loved & Appreciated!

TABLE OF CONTENTS

FOREWORD

The zeal is there to do what we have been commissioned to do but we deliberately turn a blind eye to the needs of the gospel because we don't have the financial means to support the gospel. We don't pay our tithes anymore, while those that even pay, cheat on it. In giving of our offerings, we get offended when the church is talking about giving or we don't just give at all.

In so doing, the church spends more time in talking about giving because a lot of Christians have still not caught on to the revelation of giving yet. Others have shut up their bowels of mercy and instead taken the religious route of saying "the Lord will provide" or "I will be praying for you" when they see their brother in need. The world is so tired of Christians not meeting their financial obligations. This does not bring glory to God in any way.

How can we say we are a royal priesthood but we are living like paupers? Are we governed by the economic system of this world or that of heaven? Was the curse of poverty not broken on the cross or is it a future event? Why are a lot of Christians languishing in debt when the Bible says we will be the lender and not the borrower? The author addresses all these questions in his book.

The book does not just highlight the stark reason why the author hates poverty, it goes further to tell us how we can be delivered from it forever. This book is a must read for those who want to be partakers of the Abrahamic blessing and do exploits for the Lord. The book is bold, witty, easy to read and timely. It is a book I recommend to all who want to be delivered from the bondage of poverty and those who want to be mightily used by God in these last days for the great harvest that is to come!

Emmanuel Igene

PREFACE

Despite popular perception there is absolutely nothing godly, holy or spiritual about poverty. A natural father would never wish or pray for his children to live in poverty. So, why would God?

If ye then, being evil, know how to give good gifts unto your children, how much more shall your Father which is in heaven give good things to them that ask him?

Matthew 7:11

Poverty is not just a lack of finances; it is a philosophy designed by hell to frustrate and terminate God's plan and purpose on the earth. Poverty births a grasshopper mentality, giving a myopic perspective of God. It breaks up families, cripples churches, dissolves the passion in many, and is a killer of vision. At its worst, poverty robs people of their will to live.

In this book I confront head-on misconceptions concerning prosperity and uncover an escape route from the deadly grip of poverty. Ultimately, this book is an in-depth exposé on poverty - an enemy of families, ministries, non-profit organizations, and governments.

Courage Igene

Chapter 1

WHAT IS POVERTY?

Poverty is a lack of the resources needed to complete a divine assignment. It is characterized by things of inferior quality and a pressing need for money. While poverty can be reflected in a shortage of finances and other material resources it reaches into every avenue of life, displaying itself as a lack of ideas, and a dullness in your walk with God. Poverty is not just lack of finances but a mindset that makes people settle for less. There are so many areas into which poverty reaches its destructive claws that it becomes clear why Jesus said,

> *The thief cometh not, but for to steal, and to kill, and to destroy: I am come that they might have life, and that they might have it more abundantly.*

John 10:10

Jesus came to eradicate the effects of poverty! His mission is to provide abundant life for those who will believe and receive it.

Kinds Of Poverty

(1) Poverty of the Mind: This is the inability of think outside your comfort zone. This manifests when you believe erroneously that where you are now is the furthest you will ever get, that you have no responsibility for your financial standing and that earthly things can provide you with wealth.

> *For as he thinketh in his heart, so is he…*
> **Proverbs 23:7**

Therefore, once you convince yourself of these wrong viewpoints, your life will reflect the limitations of these thoughts. For example, if you believe that you can't live at a higher level than your current status, you will be stuck in your current status. Also, if you are constantly blaming others for your financial standing and never reflect on the things you need to change, you will continue to remain at your current spot.

Likewise, if you believe your financial source is your paycheck or your friends' goodwill, instead of realizing that Jehovah is your Jireh (Provider), you will remain stranded in your current financial position. Ultimately, as long as you believe you are meant to be poor, you will remain poor.

That is, your mind's poverty will manifest itself in financial poverty. This kind of poverty, poverty of the mind, is passed on from generation to generation.

In the same way, riches can be passed from generation to generation when the mindsets taught by example in the home are positive and of the "you can do it" nature. It is said that if a person does something consistently for 21 days, a habit will be formed.

Often we think of this in terms of an actual physical task, but the same can be applied to thinking as well. As you look around at those around you who live in poverty, you will notice that many of them "think poor."

A good way to alleviate poverty of the mind is by searching the scripture. Read what the Bible says about being wealthy. As you reflect on God's word daily, you will see that he does not want you to be without or to struggle financially.

The scriptures will show you that you are a child of the most High God; it is your birthright to be prosperous and He will not let you down. Applications of God's principles guarantee your financial prosperity. Being spiritually rich does not make you financially prosperous.

(2) Spiritual Poverty: This is a lack of relationship with God. Spiritual poverty is not knowing Jesus Christ as Savior. The richest man without Jesus is poor.

> *For what shall it profit a man, if he shall gain the whole world, and lose his own soul?*

Mark 8:36

It is better to be spiritually and financially rich. Like Job…who the Bible describes as the richest man in the east.

> *…this man was the greatest of all the men of the east.*

Job 1:3

Job loved God and hated evil.

> *…and that man was perfect and upright, and one that feared God, and eschewed evil.*

Job 1:1

This verse shows that Job's relationship with God was the source of his financial prosperity.

The only way to be spiritually rich is to believe and accept the Lord Jesus Christ . Jesus in **John 14:6** tells us:

> *I am the way, the truth, and the life. No one comes to the Father except through Me.*

Once you've become spiritually rich, you will open the doors to financial prosperity.

(3) Financial Poverty: Abundant life is the very life force of God, operating in and through us, affecting everything we come in contact with. It is the blessing in us and on us that enables us to be free from the curse of poverty.

Many times, people are in poverty in some area of their lives and don't know there is a way out.

By receiving Jesus Christ, obeying the Word of God, and meditating on this important truth about abundant living, prosperity can become a reality.

I'm not just talking about having a lot of money in the bank, even though God does want us to prosper financially. I'm talking about a quality of life that is marked by an overflow of peace, health, wholeness, and provision.

In 3 John 2, the apostle Paul talks about desiring that people prosper in their spirit, soul, and body. This simply means that prosperity encompasses the physical, spiritual, and emotional realms. If someone has a lot of money but is depressed and lonely all the time, he or she is simply a poor person with a big bank account.

Or, if you are physically healthy but have bad relationships with your family and loved ones, you are a poor person with good health. To be truly prosperous, we must embrace the idea of total life prosperity. This is the will of God for all mankind, not just a select few. Jesus came to set us free from the curse of poverty so that we may live the abundant life. It is through our faith in the Word of God that this truth will become a reality in our lives.

Chapter 2

POVERTY UNMASKED

Origin Of Poverty

Poverty is a spirit that prevents you from having enough resources to fulfill a divine vision. Contrary to what many believe, there is absolutely nothing good about poverty. It may make you religious, but it certainly does not make you spiritual. If you have plans to improve your life, be a blessing to your family and community, effectively supporting the work of the Lord, then you will need a stable financial base.

In the beginning, God made man wealthy. Adam and Eve ruled creation as God's representatives. The Maker entrusted all things to the care of humanity. In fact, abundance is a theme of Genesis. That is, everything was good.

And God saw all that he had made, and behold it was very good.

Genesis 1:31a

This verse shows that in the beginning, before the fall of man, creation existed in perfect balance - humans did not lack anything good. For example, God Himself provided food (Genesis 1:29). There were no failed crops, unemployment or starving babies. There was no suffering of any kind. Adam was joyfully employed in God's garden. Work was a blessing.

In this work, humans bore God's image and glorified Him. By God's design there was no suffering or poverty. But, paradise was soon lost. Adam and Eve defied their maker and rejected His Word; they fell. The Fall brought the curse. And the curse brought poverty. Poverty is alien to God's good creation. It ought not to be. All human lack is the result of a breakdown of shalom.

In his book *State of Nothing Missing; Nothing Broken!,* Cornelius Plantinga Jr. wrote, "In the Bible, shalom means universal flourishing, wholeness, and delight – a rich state of affairs in which natural needs are satisfied and natural gifts fruitfully employed ... Shalom, in other words, is the way things ought to be." Sin is the vandalism of this peace. Man's rebellion is the ultimate source of all suffering, including economic need.

Understanding this time line, that sin is the result of man's fall and not God's original design, is crucial. This time line reveals that poverty was not God's plan or purpose for anyone. Lack, therefore, since it came as a result of mankind violating God's spiritual laws, is the opposite of God will.

Why Do So Many Associate Poverty With Godliness?

It is easy to see where the view of poverty as a form of godliness developed. First, any type of crisis usually causes a person to look for help from someone greater than him or herself. As a result, many people who are drenched in poverty exude an aura of godliness because of their consistent petitions to be alleviated of their poverty.

However, the fact that someone spends a lot of time asking God to take a crisis away, does not make the crisis God's perfect will for him or her. The crisis is not good simply because it leads the person to pray. The public's connection of poverty and piety also comes from stereotypes of wealthy people.

Wealthy people are often portrayed as arrogant, selfish, and abusive people. Though many people abuse their wealth, wealth itself is not evil. If wealth was evil, anyone who possessed it would be evil. However, millions of people choose to use their wealth in meaningful, kingdom building ways every day.

God Does Not Want You To Dwell In Poverty

Just as a loving parent would never wish poverty or any harm on their children, neither does a loving God desire anything harmful for us, the focus of His unfailing love.

Due to the corrosion of the world since the fall of humanity, poverty can come to a person from so many sources - government corruption, natural disaster, economic collapse, mishandling of money, poor choices for education, or missed opportunities.

Though the list seems endless, the root of all of them is the fact that we live in a fallen world. Despite, our presence in a fallen world, God clearly states that He does not desire His people to be poor. Though poverty comes from sin, God does not want us to remain in sin or poverty. He wants to lead us out of poverty. God is always the ever loving parent.

So, despite the fact that we are rebellious children, God does not wish us harm. He simply wishes we would repent of sin and take advantage of the wealth He has ordained us, His heirs, to possess.

God never intended for His children to live in poverty and lack. The children of the King were not created to be the "scourge of society;" they are supposed to be wealthy enough to give joyfully to help others and have enough left over to leave an inheritance for their progeny.

The scripture says;

> *A good man leaveth an inheritance to his children's children.*

Proverbs 13:22a

Jesus: The Source Of Riches

And you shall remember the Lord your God, for it is He who gives you power to get wealth, that He may establish His covenant.

Deuteronomy 8:18 (NKJV)

Because of Jesus' grace we are now able to lay hold of the many blessings, such as wealth, that God has for us. That is, God's grace, not any effort you undertake, is the source of riches. Therefore, by focusing on the blessing giver, God, instead of the blessing, riches, you have access to the fountain of riches.

This means you can be taken out of poverty and shielded from potential setbacks such as stinginess, and arrogance, because your focus is on God. That is, by loving God and realizing He is the source of wealth, you will not fall for the trap of loving money and, ultimately becoming its slave.

The great liar and deceiver Satan, has successfully fooled the world - especially believers - into believing wealth is evil. Also, Satan has convinced many that that our closeness to God is based on how poor we are. We must stand up, take back what the enemy has stolen from us, and accept the blessings of God without condemnation!

Chapter 3

SIX WAYS POVERTY OCCURS

(1) **Poverty Occurs When We Fail To Follow Divine Instruction**

Poverty and shame shall be to him that refuseth instruction: but he that regardeth reproof shall be honoured.
Proverbs 13:18

(2) **Poverty Occurs When We Become Gluttonous**

For the drunkard and the glutton shall come to poverty: and drowsiness shall clothe a man with rags.
Proverbs 23:21

(3) **Poverty Occurs When We Are Lazy**

Yet a little sleep, a little slumber, a little folding of the hands to sleep: So shall thy poverty come as one that travelleth; and thy want as an armed man."
Proverbs 24:33-34

(4) Poverty Occurs When We Make Hasty Financial Decisions (For example, when we fall for "get rich quick" schemes).

He that hasteth to be rich hath an evil eye, and considereth not that poverty shall come upon him.
Proverbs 28:22

(5) Poverty Occurs When We Refuse To Sow Financial Seeds

There is that scattereth, and yet increaseth; and there is that withholdeth more than is meet, but it tendeth to poverty.
Proverbs 11:24

(6) Poverty Occurs When We Fail Wrap Our Seed With Faith & Expect A Harvest....

One day, Peter mumbled a statement to Jesus that he and others had *"left all, and have followed thee."* Jesus did not look at him with shock asking him why he should expect anything in return; rather Jesus looked at him said;

Verily I say unto you, There is no man that hath left house, or brethren, or sisters, or father, or mother, or wife, or children, or lands, for my sake, and the gospel's, [30]But he shall receive an hundredfold now in this time, houses, and brethren, and sisters, and mothers, and children, and lands, with persecutions; and in the world to come eternal life.
Mark 10:29-30

Jesus listed what he could expect both in this life (prosperity) and the world to come. What a joy! He also said something we overlook "with persecutions" The anti-prosperity cult is a fulfillment of that. Expect to have *haters* when you are blessed beyond measure.

Dr. Mike Murdock; Founder, The Wisdom Center once said; "You are nobody until somebody hates you." The worst father on earth will never wish poverty on his children so why would our God; Owner of Silver & Gold?

The scriptures say;

> *If ye then, being evil, know how to give good gifts unto your children, how much more shall your Father which is in heaven give good things to them that ask him.*

Matthew 7:11

As Christians then, we should expect God to bless us with good gifts as we remain faithful to Him and ask him for them as we sow seeds.

Chapter 4

DELIVERANCE FROM POVERTY

God Desires To Deliver Us From Poverty

However, there should be no poor among you, *for in the land the LORD your God is giving you to possess as your inheritance, he will richly bless you.* [7]If there is a poor man among your brothers *in any of the towns of the land that the LORD your God is giving you, do not be hardhearted or tightfisted toward your poor brother.*
Deuteronomy 15:4, 7 (NIV, 1984)

This passage explains that poverty is not the plan, but rather is an anomaly. Poverty is so devastating that God endeavors to wrench us from its grip. Take a look at the following passages.

He raises the poor from the dust and lifts the needy from the ash heap; He seats them with princes and has them inherit a throne of honor.
1 Samuel 2:8

Who is like you, O LORD? You rescue the poor from those too strong for them, the poor and needy from those who rob them.
Psalm 35:10

This poor man called, and the LORD heard him; he saved him out of all his troubles.
Psalm 34:6

More Scriptures Which Reveal God's Perspective

A variety of translations are used. They give a clear picture of God's desire.

Being enriched in everything to all bountifulness, which causeth through us thanksgiving to God.
2 Corinthians 9:11 (KJV)

You will be made rich in every way so that you can be generous on every occasion, and through us your generosity will result in thanksgiving to God.
2 Corinthians 9:11 (NIV)

And God is able to make all grace abound toward you; that ye, always having all sufficiency in all things, may abound to every good work.
2 Corinthians 9:8 (KJV)

And God is able to make all grace (every favor and earthly blessing) come to me in abundance, so that I may always and under all circumstances and whatever

the need, be self-sufficient - possessing enough to require no aid or support and furnished in abundance for every good work and charitable donation."
2 Corinthians 9:8 (Amplified)

For the LORD thy God blesseth thee, as he promised thee: and thou shalt lend unto many nations, but thou shalt not borrow; and thou shalt reign over many nations, but they shall not reign over thee.
Deuteronomy 15:6 (KJV)

For the LORD your God will bless you as he has promised, and you will lend to many nations but will borrow from none. You will rule over many nations but none will rule over you.
Deuteronomy 15:6 (NIV, 1984)

And you will be called priests of the LORD, you will be named ministers of our God. You will feed on the wealth of nations, and in their riches you will boast. Instead of their shame my people will receive a double portion.
Isaiah 61:6-7

Fear the LORD; you his saints, for those who fear him lack nothing.
Psalm 34:9

Let them shout for joy, and be glad, that favour my righteous cause: yea, let them say continually, Let the LORD be magnified, which hath pleasure in the prosperity of his servant.
Psalm 35:27

This is what the LORD says, ... I will give them all the prosperity I have promised them.
Jeremiah 32:42 (NIV)

I restore your fortunes before your very eyes," says the LORD.
Zephaniah 3:20 (NIV)

A sinner's wealth is stored up for the righteous.
Proverbs. 13:22 (NIV)

Blessed is the man who fears the Lord; wealth and riches will be in his house.
Psalm 112:1,3 (NKJV)

As for the rich in this world, charge them not to be proud and arrogant and contemptuous of others, nor to set their hopes on uncertain riches, but on God, Who richly and ceaselessly provides us with everything for [our] enjoyment.
1 Timothy 6:17 (Amplified)

These verses of Scriptures above show that poverty is a crisis, a pit from which we must be saved. God alone has the power to deliver us from this hole.

The above Scriptures do not suggest a God who wants His children to suffer and live in lack. Rather, these verses show that wealth is a blessing God intends to shower on all of His children.

Chapter 5

MONEY: THE TRUTH AND THE LIES

In all my years of preaching, conducting Healing Rain crusades, hosting weekly live nationwide telephone prayer conferences, and speaking at revivals and conventions, many have come to me for prayer. The number one prayer request is for finances.

Over the years, as I have prayed with people who experience financial troubles I have consistently noticed that their belief systems contain one or more of the following four lies about finances. These erroneous beliefs have directly affected their financial status, either leading them to poverty or keeping them trapped in poverty.

Four Lies Many Believe About Finances

(1) Money Is The Root of All Evil: Your parents, pastor or someone else significant in your life may have passed this or similar beliefs to you either directly or indirectly through their attitudes to people and events.

These beliefs stem from a misrepresentation of Apostle Paul's statement in Timothy:

> *For the love of money is the root of all evil...*
>
> **1 Timothy 6:10**

This verse does not say that money is evil; it says that the *love of*, or obsession with money is the root or beginning of evil. This is because the love of money is *idolatry*. It is the worship of the creation instead of the Creator. A clear distinction must be made between *the love* of money and money itself. God is not anti-money, or anti-wealth, He is anti-money worship.

Consequently, He has helped us to identify that money love (worship) is the root of all kinds of evil. God owns all money.

> *The silver is Mine, and the gold is Mine, saith the Lord of hosts.*
>
> **Haggai 2:8**

As we discussed before, God has given us money as a gift. Because we know that God would never give us, His children, a bad gift, we know that money must be good. The fact that people often misuse money does not undermine the goodness of the gift (or of the Gift Giver). For example, fire destroys homes, beautiful forests and kills human beings. Yet, properly controlled, it is a tremendous tool for cooking food, warming houses and running automobile engines.

Just like fire, water has caused destruction of property and lives. Yet, water is necessary for every day human life. Also, plants and animals flourish wherever there is a consistent source of water. So it is with money. Though money has the potential to be used to serve harmful purposes, money's true purpose, as a gift from God, is to serve the kingdom.

The Apostle Paul explains this purpose saying;

> *You will be made rich in every way so that you can be generous on every occasion, and through us your generosity will result in thanksgiving to God.*
> **2 Corinthians 9:11 (NIV)**

With this statement, Paul declares that wealth is good. Money is a kingdom blessing every kingdom member is supposed to receive. As one comedian has said, "Money is not cold, hard cash, but warm, soft blessings!"

(2) Some Are Destined For Wealth And Some Are Destined For Poverty: This absurd lie has destroyed initiative, drive and motivation in many would-be winners throughout the world. Many capable people have believed the song: "Whatever will be, will be" "Whatever *is,* was *meant* to be." The truth is, through development of your God-given *talents* and the principles of *giving* and *obedience* you determine the financial Harvest of your life. First, your financial status will depend on your willingness to work and develop the talents and assets God has given you.

Hard work means prosperity; only a fool idles away his time...Work hard and become a leader; be lazy and never succeed.
Proverbs 12:11, 24 (TLB)

Also

Work brings profit.
Proverbs 14:23a (TLB)

Second, you will need to develop a lifestyle of giving. Jesus said:

Give, and it shall be given unto you...
Luke 6:38

Solomon said:

There is that scattereth, and yet increaseth; and there is that withholdeth more than is meet, but it tendeth to poverty. [25]The liberal soul shall be made fat: and he that watereth shall be watered also himself.
Proverbs 11:24-25

Thus, in order to retain and build wealth, you will have to sow abundantly and responsibly the wealth God has given you. This includes paying your tithes and offerings. To those who do not responsibly give to God's house, God says;

Ye are cursed with a curse; for ye have robbed Me.
Malachi 3:9a

Finally, you will need to be obedient to God's instructions. God explained that financial curses or blessing depend on your level of *obedience*. In Deuteronomy 28, God lists all the blessings that will follow if one is obedient; He includes various forms of financial wealth in the list. In contrast, God listed a number of curses that would follow disobedience - various types of poverty are on that list.

(3) Money Is Not A Spiritual Subject And Should Not Be Mentioned In Church: This belief is preposterous. Some people spend at least forty hours a week working hard for money, yet they get angry if a man of God tells them for fifteen minutes that God wants to prosper them financially. As a result of this erroneous belief, money is the great "Silent Subject" in many churches.

That is, there is very little teaching on financial prosperity from the pulpit. Also, very few churches provide training on how to implement biblical principles into one's daily financial life. Yet, there are profound practical and spiritual reasons why the church should be regularly teaching and training its people on Biblical principles of financial stewardship.

Finances and Discipleship

(I) Money is a Spiritual Issue

Our main guide to which matters are spiritual in nature is the Bible. 11 out of the 39 parables are about money. Therefore, money is a spiritual matter simply because Jesus devoted a significant amount of time to teaching about finances. Jesus' lessons establish that our attitude and relationship to money is a key discipleship issue. A person's relationship to his or her money and "stuff" is often a barrier to spiritual growth and development. Wealth is, for many *the* rival god.

Money is also a key component of the Christian call to discipleship in other ways. For instance, our handling of money as stewards, our giving of money in sacrifice, and the appropriate avenues of wealth accumulation are all key discipleship issues.

(II) The Teaching Challenge

As important as the issue of money is, many pastors and church leaders are challenged and conflicted when it comes to teaching and preaching about it. There are various reasons for this:

> ➢ **Lack of Financial Knowledge:** The only part of the Bible that works for you is the part you know. Many church leaders do not have financial knowledge. They do not know the Bible's teachings on finances. As a result, they can't teach about finances in a meaningful way.

➢ **Lack of Affinity toward Money:** Many have been taught that when you talk about money, you are greedy and selfish. Therefore, many pastors are not "wired" to have an interest in money or monetary issues. Thus, because they don't respect money, they rarely, if ever, speak about it. They may also inadvertently pass on their disrespect of money to their congregants, spreading the erroneous view that money is not a spiritual matter.

➢ **Personal Financial Issues:** When people are struggling financially, they lack the tenacity and courage to talk to others about their finances. So, Christian teachers who do not have stable finances often forget their anointing is not for them but for others. As a result of their insecurity with their own finances, they neglect to teach others the Word's principles on the issue.

➢ **A Resistant Culture:** The predominant cultural view is that finances are out of the church's teaching scope. Instead of fighting this view and teaching the Word, the church has often been overwhelmed with the world's view.

Money is a major part of our daily lives. The minister is responsible for establishing the balance believers should have when it comes to finances. While money *lovers* must be warned, the *givers* should be *encouraged*.

The Church is called to explain the role money should play in everyday life.

But, most importantly, The Church should teach about money's role in worship. For example, the church should explain that offering time is worship time - a time to minister unto God's kingdom and sow into our own future. The Church should not let the cynical prevailing world views on finances dilute your revelation on financial blessing.

(4) Money Will Make You Backslide: Wearing the mask of false humility, someone once approached me at the end of a meeting with a proud, Pharisee swagger and proclaimed, "All this prosperity teaching…Money will make you backslide, you know!" His blatant ignorance and desire to advertise it appalled me. I simply replied, "So, how come you don't have it? If money will make you backslide, why hasn't the devil overdosed you with it?"

He looked puzzled and slowly responded, "Wow that is so true…never crossed my mind." The Bible makes this point most clearly when explaining Job's test. When the devil wanted to strike Job and disconnect him from God, the devil did not double Job's finances, rather he cut them off (Job 1).

Prosperity Is A Magnifier

Financial Prosperity only magnifies who you really are. If you possess the giving nature of God, prosperity magnifies it. On the other hand, if you are stingy or, like one of my friends would say, "refusing to drop a dollar till it holla," then prosperity will reveal your stinginess. Prosperity is the great magnifier in other ways.

It will also reveal if you love the work of God and people. If you backslide after God blesses you financially, you were always susceptible to backsliding. The money did not cause you to backslide, it simply exposed that weakness in you. Backsliding is an issue of the heart and character not financial standing.

Incentive For Obedience

God has never been and will never be against you having finances; He just does not want your finances to own you. No wonder He constantly offered financial prosperity as an incentive for obedience (Deuteronomy 28:1-14, Proverbs 3:9-10, Luke 6:38).

Building The Kingdom

It baffles me that many believe God wants them to live in poverty. They argue that as long as they have a roof over their head and can feed their children, they are fine.

This mindset is myopic and self-centered. When people insist that simply having enough to put a roof over their heads is all God wants them to have, they make no mention of helping others, sponsoring children through school, helping widows in need, or partnering with Ministries preaching the Gospel of the Kingdom.

Thus, with this mindset, they limit their responsibilities as Christians. By simply accepting a roof over their heads, they can never fully step up to their duty to take care of the church, the kingdom and the world at large. This mindset also ignores the fact that Christ's sacrifice on the cross freed us from all bondage including that of poverty.

> *For ye know the grace of our Lord Jesus Christ, that, though he was rich, yet for your sakes he became poor, that ye through his poverty might be rich.*

2 Corinthians 8:9

This wealth we have received through Christ's sacrifice is supposed to be used to build God's kingdom here on earth. When wealthy believers use their wealth to reach others with the Gospel of the Kingdom, they are laying up treasures in Heaven.

Jesus said;

> *Do not lay up for yourselves treasures on earth, where moth and rust destroy and where thieves break in and steal;*

[20]but lay up for yourselves treasures in heaven, where neither moth nor rust destroys and where thieves do not break in and steal.

Matthew 6:19-20

The Apostle Paul expressed the same principle by writing;

Command those who are rich in this present age not to be haughty, nor to trust in uncertain riches but in the living God, who gives us richly all things to enjoy. [18]Let them do good, that they be rich in good works, ready to give, willing to share, [19]storing up for themselves a good foundation for the time to come, that they may lay hold on eternal life.

1 Timothy 6:17-19

Rather than condemn the rich or wealth in general Paul, who himself was a man of means, instructed rich Christians to utilize their vast wealth for what it was intended: ministry. Paul did not tell the rich Christians to feel guilty for being wealthy, or to trade their wealth for poverty, so that they would be better Christians.

Instead, he urged them to use their money for God's purposes. Without Christians with some serious money, the followers of Christ would have to depend on the worldly wealthy who hate or do not know Christ. What sense does it make to put the church in a position where it is dependent on the unsaved to finance God's work?

Chapter 6

THE ANTICS OF THE
ANTI-PROSPERITY CULT

S atan is more conscious of the more than 3 billion people in this world who need salvation than most Christians are. So, he opposes anything good and works tirelessly to spread the message that wealth is bad. Why else would anyone in their right mind be anti-blessing, anti-divine provision and supernatural supply? It's not natural to hate provision; this is why you should know that the forces of hell are behind anyone who fights something Jesus died to give you.

Satan is raising up an "anti-prosperity cult" and he plans on fooling you with it. His mantra is "The less you have the holier you are." Satan labors diligently to convince believers that poverty means you are holy, though the Bible says poverty is a curse for being a fool. Satan also wants people to believe that only a small handful of individuals are supposed to prosper.

When the body of Christ accepts this type of thinking, this philosophy stops members from praying for the finances to save the lost people of the world.

Therefore, it is vital that we reject these false notions and demonic, prideful lies.

Our loving Father wants our lives to be a testimony of wealth and health. That way when we set out to seek and to save the lost, destroying the works of Satan in the process, we will be heard and not scorned.

Poverty Is A Vision Killer

Poverty is to be despised because God despises poverty. God denounces poverty because it kills the dreams he has given His Creation. When God's creation is mired in poverty, it often fails to fully meet its God given purpose of reaching the lost people of the world.

The scripture says;

> *A needy man's dreams are fractured by his poverty.*
> **Proverbs 10:15b**

Poverty is a hothouse where seeds of hopelessness, suicide, fear, anger and resentment of God grow and bloom. For instance, poverty causes people to live in fear, unsure of their futures and the respect of others. Poverty also leads many to question the goodness of God.

Whenever God puts a big dream in someone's heart to use his or her gifts and anointing to win the world to Christ, Satan is challenged. He moves immediately to kill that dream, often using poverty.

Satan tries to convince them that poverty would be a better route. He tells them that the poorer they are, the holier they are; Satan lies in this way because he knows Ecclesiastes chapter nine better than most Christians do.

> *Then said I, Wisdom is better than strength: nevertheless the poor man's wisdom is despised, and his words are not heard.*

Ecclesiastes 9:16

Satan knows that the Bible says that nobody will listen to the preaching of a poor man. Satan understands that a poor man's words are met with skepticism. The impoverished preacher's audience thinks, "If you're so bright, how come you ain't got nothing? If your God is worth serving, how come He doesn't give you a better pair of shoes?" That is Satan's dream, to shut up preachers by putting them in position where nobody will listen to them.

Freeing The Captives

Those who resist and reject prosperity cite the sufferings of Paul and the early church as proof that the Gospel of Christ is contrary to prosperity. But this line of argument reveals an incorrect conflation of persecution with poverty.

Christians have always been and will still be persecuted for their faith in Christ.

Saying that Christians will be persecuted for spreading the message of hope is not the same as saying God intends for Christians to live in poverty.

One passage that clarifies the issue is **Mark 10:28-30**:

> *...Then Peter began to say unto him, lo, we have left all, and have followed thee. ²⁹and Jesus answered and said, Verily I say unto you, There is no man that hath left house, or brethren, or sisters, or father, or mother, or wife, or children, or lands, for my sake, and the gospel's, ³⁰But he shall receive an hundredfold now in this time, houses, and brethren, and sisters, and mothers, and children, and lands, with persecutions; and in the world to come eternal life.*

In the above passage, Peter responds to Jesus' warning that it will be difficult for those who trust in riches to receive salvation. Peter's statement to Jesus is not proof that in order to follow Jesus you have to be poor, rather Peter uses it to prove to Jesus that he and the other disciples have not trusted in riches. That is, Peter's response can be paraphrased as, "Jesus we don't trust in riches, we proved this by leaving everything we have to serve you. What will be our reward?"

Jesus replied not in shock, but with reassurance, promising not only salvation and eternal life. Jesus also mentioned two other distinct things followers could expect: riches in *this* life and persecutions. Thus, Jesus explains that the persecution of which He speaks is not poverty. Christians, Jesus explains, can expect to be rewarded with more than they could ever give physically and spiritually in their service to Christ.

This reward will be a hundredfold return for everything they invest in the kingdom. So, though Christ expects Christians to constantly be giving for the sake of the gospel, He also expects them to live in abundance as their reward for dedicating their lives and finances to the gospel.

The idea that Christians are meant to live in abundance is bolstered by **Luke 4:18-19 (NIV, 1984)** where it is recorded that Jesus read from the book of Isaiah:

> *The Spirit of the Lord is on me, because he has anointed me to preach good news to the poor. He has sent me to proclaim freedom for the prisoners and recovery of sight for the blind, to release the oppressed, [19] to proclaim the year of the Lord's favor.*

After that, He sat down and said "Today this scripture is fulfilled in your hearing." What exactly is the "good news to the poor" which Jesus was anointed to preach? That the poor will remain poor? What's so good about that? Jesus also says in John 10:10 that He came to give us a more abundant life.

It's not possible that when Jesus promised good news for the poor and an abundant life for His followers, that He intended his followers to wallow in poverty.

Christ proclaims that He frees Christians from captivity, including that of poverty. This freedom is the root of the message of the gospel. That is, with the freedom access to wealth brings, Christians can better spread the Gospel.

For example, churches can be run by full time ministers. Currently, many ministers who believe the anti-prosperity cult struggle to make ends meet and often work other jobs while juggling their responsibilities as a pastor. As a result, their pastoral work often suffers. Churches that can afford to pay full-time staff, not just a pastor often have the best chance of spreading the gospel to amazing distances.

That is, with their funding they can disseminate the Gospel through the mass media of literature, radio, television, and the Internet. Ironically though, many churches that decry the idea of a prosperous body of Christ actually devote a lot of time appealing for money, or selling their books, CDs, and DVDs in attempts to raise funds. While these Christians frantically try to raise money to carry out their God given assignment, they speak against the importance of money in getting God's work done. This presents a colossal irony: these Christians raise millions of dollars to construct church complexes, operate Christian media (radio, television, Internet), and run Christian schools while simultaneously condemning those who proclaim the importance of finances in the kingdom.

Divine Prosperity In Biblical Patriarchs And Matriarchs

As the Bible describes various Godly men and women, it notes that these people were extremely wealthy. The following is a list of people who had enormous wealth at their disposal.

(1) The patriarchs of faith (Abraham, Isaac, Jacob, Joseph) were all wealthy.

(2) All the Godly kings of Israel and Judah were wealthy.

(3) Then there were Godly wealthy people like Boaz (husband of Ruth), Daniel, and Esther, among others.

(4) After reading about New Testament Christians, it becomes obvious that there were very wealthy Christians in the first-century churches. Among them were Cornelius, Lydia, and many others. They used their resources, becoming partners with the Apostles and spreading Gospel of the Kingdom throughout the Roman Empire.

Chapter 7

THE BATTLE OVER YOUR EXPECTATION

Expect To Receive From God

Your seed is something you sow to bless others; your harvest is what you reap to bless yourself so that you can continue to be a blessing. Your expectation that your sowing will lead to a harvest is faith. Your faith gives God pleasure. God loves to be trusted and believed. Haters of prosperity messages are not really against giving.

What they fiercely criticize is anyone who talks about the ability of Jehovah-Jireh to bless you in return for the seeds you've sown into the work of God. They argue it is greed to expect something back from your seed. Their argument is in part based on a confusion of the words expectation and purpose.

If you *only* give so that you can receive from God, that is greed. However, if when you give, you know that God can bless you more than you can possibly bless others, that is expectation.

This expectation is the nutrient that makes your seed bring forth a harvest.

Why The Battle Over Your Expectation?

God said it is absolutely impossible to please Him unless we expect something from Him.

> *But without faith, it is impossible to please Him: for He that cometh to God must believe that He is, and that He is a rewarder of them that diligently seek Him.*

Hebrews 11:6

Let's carefully review these questions:

(1) When you gave your life to Christ, did you expect forgiveness for your sin?

Of course you did. This is why you are saved today. What if the preacher told you: "as you surrender to Jesus, please don't expect forgiveness, or your sins to be washed away, don't expect your name written in the Book of Life, don't expect to now become the righteousness of God in Christ Jesus? It's greed to expect something back for confessing your sins." I guarantee you would say: "then what's the point? Why surrender in the first place?"

(2) Do you expect a paycheck from your job every two weeks?

I doubt that your paycheck comes to you as a shock. This is because you are getting something in return for your seed of time and service sown. Do you tell your boss: "Oh never mind paying me, I work here because I love you guys so much?" I doubt it!

(3) When you bring your sick body to Jesus, do you expect Him to heal you?

Of course you do. The list goes on. It's only expecting a financial harvest that causes a stir. This is not natural. Of all the doctrines in the Bible, hatred is centered on a principle that brings blessing, provision, ability to be a blessing to others and get the gospel to the ends of the earth. This tells you it's satanic. Anytime satan stops your expectation, he has succeeded in killing the only pleasure God derives from your life. Your expectation creates a river of pleasure in the heart of God. The anti-prosperity cult is against you expecting a financial harvest from God. Why would anyone spend precious time sneering men of God praying for people to come out of poverty?

When you add "Expectation of a return" you arouse every demon in hell. Why do many get angry over expectation of a harvest? Because they don't believe in reaping a harvest from their seed. They have been taught to expect nothing in return. If you believed you would receive one hundred fold return from your seed sown, offering time would excite you.

You won't say: "Oh, they have come again!" According to the Bible, every time God required an offering, He always attached a harvest to anyone who obeyed. God longs to be believed so much He offered financial prosperity as an incentive for obedience. This is because you cannot out give God. He is a giver.

Let's Examine These Scriptures

(1) *God so loved the world that He gave his only begotten son, that* **whosoever believes in him should not perish but have everlasting life.**
John 3:16

We see God as the ultimate giver who gave His best and a harvest of everlasting life is promised to as many that will dare to believe Him.

(2) *Give and it shall be given back to you; good measure, pressed down, shaken together, running over shall men give unto your bosom. For with the same measure that ye mete withal it shall be measured to you again.*
Luke 6:38

The above scripture explains seven levels of receiving for giving once. We see how God offers overflow to motivate you to sow a seed. You can't beat God giving. Praise God!

Say To Yourself:

I am a receiver of everything God has for me!

(3) Honor the LORD with thy substance and with the first fruits of thine increase; [10]*So shall thy barns be filled with plenty, and thy presses shall burst out with new wine.*

Proverbs 3:9-10

Here we see a picture of overflowing barns as a harvest for honoring the LORD with your substance.

(4) Bring ye all the tithes into the storehouse, that there may be meat in mine house, and prove me now herewith, saith the LORD of hosts, if I will not open you the windows of heaven, and pour you out a blessing, that **there shall not be room enough to receive it**. [11]*And I will rebuke the devourer for your sakes, and he shall not destroy the fruits of your ground; neither shall your vine cast her fruit before the time in the field, saith the LORD of hosts.* [12]*And all nations shall call you blessed: for ye shall be a delightsome land, saith the LORD of hosts.*

Malachi 3:10-12

This is the only scripture God dares us to prove He exists. He says if we bring Him the tithe, it will create provision for His Work on earth and at the same time, He will swing to action for us by opening the windows of Heaven, pour us a blessing and the blessing goes on. What a supernatural supply reserved for those who dares to believe the God of abundance! Will you?

*(5) And it shall come to pass, if thou shalt hearken diligently unto the voice of the LORD thy God, to observe **and** to do all his commandments which I command thee this day, that the LORD thy God will set thee on high above all nations of the*

earth: And all these blessings shall come on thee, and overtake thee, if thou shalt hearken unto the voice of the LORD thy God…..

Deuteronomy 28:1-14

The above scripture shows a list of untold blessings in store for those that will obey God. Why would God give us these portraits of prosperity? To inspire us to obey Him. For example: One day, Peter mumbled a statement that he and others had *left all, and have followed thee.*

Jesus did not look at him with shock asking him why he should expect anything in return; rather Jesus responded to him:

> *Verily I say unto you, There is no man that hath left house, or brethren, or sisters, or father, or mother, or wife, or children, or lands, for my sake, and the gospel's,* ³⁰*But he shall receive an hundredfold now in this time, houses, and brethren, and sisters, and mothers, and children, and lands, with persecutions; and in the world to come eternal life.*
> **Mark 10:29-30**

Jesus listed what he could expect (including prosperity) both in this life and the world to come. What a joy! He also said something we overlook "with persecutions." The anti-prosperity cult is a fulfillment of that. Expect to have haters when you are blessed beyond measure. You are insignificant when you have nothing, but the moment God begins to do business on earth through you; you immediately provoke joy and blessing robbers wearing religious masks.

Never forget you are nobody until somebody hates you. Giving is the only cure for greed, not hoarding. Whenever you sow to get a harvest, you have just conquered greed. When you sow with expectation, your seed will come before God as photograph of your faith. Master the habit of sowing from every paycheck, sow expectantly, generously and consistently and expect the God of the universe to fulfill His promise.

Trust God & Always Expect To

(A) Receive answers to your prayers.

(B) Receive healing for your physical bodies.

(C) Prosper.

(D) Grow spiritually.

(E) Live victoriously over sin and temptation.

(F) Experience revival and win souls for Christ.

(G) Overcome trials and tribulations.

(H) Accomplish the impossible.

(I) Appropriate any other promises and benefits that God has revealed to you.

(J) Make it to heaven.

Chapter 8

REASONS GOD WANTS YOU TO BE WEALTHY

Reason #1

God Loves You So Much That It Pleasures Him When You Have Financial Success.

Let them shout for joy, and be glad, that favor my righteous cause: yea, let them say continually, Let the LORD be magnified, which hath pleasure in the prosperity of His servant.

Psalm 35:27

God wants nothing but the best for you. He loves you and delights in you. When you're comfortable and happy, He is especially happy. God made humans so He could share His love with them. In the first chapter of Genesis, the first time He mentioned humans, He talked about making them just like Him.

> *And God said; Let us make man in our image, after our likeness: and let them have dominion over the fish of the sea, and over the fowl of the air, and over the cattle, and over all the earth, and over every creeping thing that creeps upon the earth.*

Genesis 1:26

Without hesitation God made you to be just like Himself and gave you dominion. Your financial success is so important to God that He planned for your wealth when He was creating the earth.

Let's look at **Genesis 1:11-12**;

> *And God said let the earth bring forth grass, the herb yielding seed, and the fruit tree yielding fruit after his kind, whose seed is in itself, upon the earth: and it was so. ¹²And the earth brought forth grass and herb yielding seed after his kind, and the tree yielding fruit, whose seed was in itself, after his kind: and God saw that it was good.*

This passages show that when God was creating the earth, He set up a system which induced increase. Every plant already had seeds (the first thing needed to reproduce) in itself, establishing a process that would continuously produce food. In **Genesis 1:29**, God goes a step further, explaining the system to humans and giving them power over the system.

And God said, Behold, I have given you every herb bearing seed, which is upon the face of all the earth, and every tree, in the which is the fruit of a tree yielding seed; to you it shall be for meat.

According to the scripture above, God was dedicated to providing humanity with more than enough to meet their needs and desires.

You can see God's delight in Job's life.

And the Lord said unto Satan, Hast though considered my servant Job, tat there is none like him in the earth, a perfect and an upright man, one that feareth God and escheweth evil?

Job 1:8

God was excited about Job's spiritual and financial wealth and made sure both were recorded in the Bible (Job 1:1-3 lists Jobs considerable financial assets). Even when Job lost all his wealth because of his fear, God restored Job's wealth, wanting to ensure both Jobs spiritual and financial upliftment.

Abraham's life also shows how much God wants to share His love towards us. God told Abraham to leave his family and go to a land that He was going to show him. When times got tough, Abraham disobeyed God and went to Egypt. Abraham became fearful of Pharaoh and said that Sarah was his sister to avoid any attack from Pharaoh.

Pharaoh then took Sarah and gave Abraham riches. Because Pharaoh took Abraham's wife, trouble began to hit Pharaoh's palace. Pharaoh figured that it must be Sarah that was causing the problems, so Pharaoh questioned Abraham about Sarah. Eventually Abraham told Pharaoh that Sarah was his wife. Pharaoh immediately told Abraham to take his wife, gather his things and leave. But, Pharaoh did not ask Abraham to return the stuff he had given to Abraham. So, Abraham left Egypt with all these possessions (Genesis 12:9-20).

Some people think Abraham received the blessing of God, but, really Abraham received the mercy of God. The blessing of God can't operate in disobedience. However, God loved Abraham so much that even though Abraham disobeyed God, God's still showed mercy, allowing Abraham to be wealthy.

Reason #2

God Wants To Use You As a Showcase of His Fatherhood!

Throughout the Bible, God has used people to display how awesome a father He is. For example, He used Abraham, Isaac, Job, and Solomon. More importantly, He wants to use you!

Most people are moved by what they see and not what they hear from the Word of God. So, God wants you to display His workmanship in your life. When He uses your life as an example, your family, coworkers, and friends see how good God is.

When others see you living in abundance, the inaccurate, traditional mean god image is destroyed and the God of love, God's true nature, is introduced. When He was here on earth, Jesus didn't draw attention simply because He was God's son. Jesus drew attention because everywhere He went lack dissipated! The first miracle performed by Jesus (John 2:1-11) addressed lack. Jesus and His family went to a wedding. When the hosts ran out of wine, Mary, Jesus' mother, told Him.

Jesus told them to fill barrels with water, within seconds, Jesus then turned that water into wine. Let's appreciate this miracle. Though good wine takes years to make, Jesus made His in seconds (The closest we can come in seconds is Kool Aid!). The guests proclaimed that it was the best wine in the party. Jesus destroyed lack, in a tremendous way.

Throughout His earthly ministry, Jesus continued to do this over and over again. For instance, Jesus provided money to pay taxes by having money miraculously appear in a fish's mouth (Luke 17:26). Jesus also fed over 5000 people with only five loaves of bread and two small fish (John 6:1-14).

He also fed over 400 people with seven loaves bread and a few small fish. (Mark 8: 6-8). In both cases when he fed people, there was enough to feed everyone present and create leftovers.

That same lack destroying power displayed by the Son of God is also available to you as a child of God. Once you expect God to destroy lack in your life and bless your finances abundantly, He will. As a result, people will be attracted to you. When they are attracted to you, you will simply have to direct their attention to your loving Father who has provided these blessings. Therefore as you prosper, God's abilities as a Father will be showcased.

Reason #3

God Wants To Keep His Promise To You!

God is all about keeping promises. In Genesis 12:3, God promised to make all the families of the earth blessed. God doesn't ever forget what He says or promises. That's why you must understand the word covenant. If you don't grasp the concept of covenant, then you will never be able to understand how to reap the abundant financial success God is offering.

Let's define covenant. A covenant is a binding agreement. God promises to take care of us, in return God expects us to serve Him. God promises not simply to provide a roof over our heads, but to bless us abundantly.

The scriptures say;

> *And my God shall supply all your needs according to His riches in glory in Christ Jesus.*
>
> **Philippians 4:19**

This means that God is going to provide a supply that meets the standards of *His* riches and glory. Therefore the supply of wealth we should expect from God is supernatural. In response to this abundant supply, God expects us to be faithful. Moses reminded the people of this covenant by saying,

> *But thou shall remember the LORD thy **God:** for it is He that gives thee power to get wealth, that He may establish His Covenant which he swore unto thy fathers, as it is this day.*
>
> **Deuteronomy 8:18**

Chapter 9

GIVING ENHANCES YOUR HOLINESS AND SPIRITUALITY

There was an evangelistic team who traveled 600 miles one way to get to a church. Their bus got only ten miles per gallon of fuel. In addition to spending $150.00 for fuel, this party of twelve had some sandwiches on their way. At the end of their ministry in the destination church, sinners were converted and many were healed. The pastor decided to receive a love offering for the guests.

When announcing the offering, he told the congregation that he didn't even know if this party of twelve needed it. Handing the $65.00 that came in the offering to the leader of the team, the pastor told the ministry leader that he would have to answer to God for how the ministry spent the offering. The pastor's actions reflect the church's general skepticism about giving to ministers.

Often Christians become a blessing to a congregation; souls are saved from hell and lives are healed and transformed.

These Christians are often not blessed financially by the churches to which they minister. Usually, these churches simply send these ministers on their way with a "God bless you." Some churches even teach that it is wrong to sow into the life of these ministers.

Paul's teachings show that these beliefs are wrong. In the following verse he commends early Christians for their dedication to sowing into ministry.

> *For I know the forwardness of your mind, for which I boast of you to them of Macedonia, that Achaia was ready a year ago; and your zeal hath provoked very many. ³Yet have I sent the brethren, lest our boasting of you should be in vain in this behalf; that, as I said, ye may be ready:*

2 Corinthians 9:2-3

The Holiness Of Giving

On another ministry event, the same ministry group was in another church which was packed with people, who claimed they were a holiness church. One man in the church had on a pair of $1700.00 cowboy boots. Yet, the pastor had to try three times in order to raise an offering of $100.00. These people who professed high holiness standards needed to be taught that giving is part of holiness. A very definite law of God and of life in general is that we will reap according to how we sow.

Every man according as he purposeth in his heart, so let him give; not grudgingly, or of necessity: for God loveth a cheerful giver.

2 Corinthians 9:7

Some will use the above verse to say that God does not require a tenth of your earnings. This chapter is not talking about tithing, but about giving. The word *cheerful* actually comes from a Greek word from which we get our word hilarious. Therefore the verse explains that it is fun to give. It is even profitable to give. In Acts this point is emphasized through the statement:

It is more blessed to give than to receive.

Acts 20:35b

As it is written, He hath dispersed abroad; (missions) *he hath given to the poor:* (helping the needy) ***his righteousness remaineth for ever.***

2 Corinthians 9:9

Notice that the man who gives is counted righteous. The next verse delves further:

Now he that ministereth seed to the sower both minister bread for your food, and multiply your seed sown, and increase (notice that word increase) the fruits of your righteousness.

2 Corinthians 9:10

Therefore the scriptures establish that giving is righteous. Additionally, the more you give, the more your righteousness. That is, your gifts are increased because God multiplies your gifts.

Remember, if your 'holiness' does not extend to your finances, it is lacking.

Chapter 10

LAWS THAT GUARANTEE YOUR WEALTH

Thou hast caused men to ride over our heads; we went through fire and through water: but thou broughtest us out into a wealthy [place].

Psalm 66:12

The gospel has two parts. One is the person of Jesus and the other is the laws of God. The person of Jesus creates your peace and prepares you for heaven while the laws create your prosperity here on earth. There are laws that guarantee wealth.

Here Are The Top Laws

(1) The Law of Priority

Seek ye first the kingdom of God and His righteousness, and all these things shall be added to you.
Matthew 6:33

For the eyes of the LORD run to and fro throughout the whole earth, to show Himself strong in behalf of those whose hearts are fully committed to Him.

2 Chronicles 16:9

Passionately pursue your relationship with God. The master key to the blessed life is to seek God first and not money or things. As you love, honor and obey God, prioritizing Him, you'll become a magnet for God's favor.

(2) The Law of Responsibility...*Responsibility for your decisions.*

Diligently follow the words of this covenant, and do them, that you may prosper in all that you do.

Deuteronomy 29:9

*If you are willing and obedient, you will enjoy the **best** of the land.*

Isaiah 1:19

Avoid the victim mentality and get out of the blame game! It's your life—take full responsibility for it! *Stop blaming* the government, the IRS, your race, your family background, the economy, your job, your lack of education, your church, your in-laws or anything else for your lot in life. As long as you blame others, you surrender your power to change. When you finally stop playing the victim, you will open the pathway to becoming a victor.

(3) The Law of Vision

And be renewed in the spirit of your mind.

Ephesians 4:23

Develop a winner's mentality. Renew your mind in the Word of God and choose to see yourself the way God sees you! Erase negative, defeatist, and mediocre mindsets. Refuse to be accept small dreams.

As he thinketh in his heart, so is he.

Proverbs 23:7

Your life won't change until your thoughts change. Our state of mind always creates our state of results. When we change what we think, we change what we attract. Harness the power of accurate thinking.

Some just can't see themselves doing great things for God. They don't see themselves building hospitals or churches, orphanages, homes for the homeless, sponsoring missionaries, or doing anything of worth for the kingdom. As a result, they don't.

(4) The Law of Focus

Write the vision and make it plain on tablets, that he may run who reads it.

Habakkuk 2:2

My heart is fixed, O God, my heart is fixed…

Psalm 57:7

...but this one thing I do, forgetting those things which are behind, and reaching forth unto those things which are before.
Philippians 3:13

You move in the direction you are facing. Without a vision and without goals you are going to sink. Your vision is your future, while goals are the starting point of all success. Goals are a to-do-list with a deadline. Having goals and a clear focus puts purpose and passion in your life.

It's unfortunate many Christians today have no focus. One unbeliever with a goal will do greater things than a believer without one. Men fail because of a lack of focus. As they become distracted, they are unable to focus on the important and reach success. A famous billionaire once said "the difference between me and others is people try too many things every day, but I focus on one."

(5) The Law of Discovery

Everything you have always wanted has already arrived. It is just awaiting your recognition of it. A poor couple in 1800s sold their home and went to Europe to look for gold. When they returned home, they noticed their house was fenced in by Government Security. The government had found the largest gold mine in the North American Peninsula on their property.

May God open your eyes today to discover your hidden riches in Jesus name!

➤ Discovery of a gift God has placed in you...

A man's gift makes room for him, and brings him before great men.
Proverbs 18:16

➤ Discovery of a Divine Instruction...

Many have not understood that most times divine instructions arrive camouflaged as a suggestion. So, many miss the entry to their wealthy place because they fail to recognize that God is instructing them.

➤ Discovery of a God Opportunity...

God never told David to kill Goliath. David simply discovered an opportunity to reap a harvest. David asked what would be given to the man that kills the giant. In other words what can I expect as my harvest if I kill this giant? He was told he won't have to pay taxes the rest of his life and would marry the king's daughter. David said to himself, "That sounds like a pretty good harvest to me." He then seized the moment.

➤ Discovery of A Divine Destiny Helper...

And a certain man found him, *and, behold, he was wandering in the field: and the man asked him, saying, What seekest thou?* [16]*And he said, I seek my brethren: tell me, I pray thee, where they feed their flocks.*[17]*And the man said, They are departed hence; for I heard them say, Let us go to Dothan. And Joseph went after his brethren, and found them in Dothan.*
Genesis 37:15-17

While Joseph was looking for his brothers, a certain man showed up and helped him find them. We see this destiny helper enabled Joseph to locate his brothers.

➤ Discovery of a Man of God In Your Life…

Many have missed God because they did not know how to honor or receive the prophet of their destiny. They trivialized his words, ignored his instruction and despised the anointing and grace on his or her life.

2 Chronicles 20:20 declares:

> *Believe in the LORD your God, so shall ye be established; believe his prophets, so shall ye prosper.*

So, if you are not prospering, you should make sure you are not defying the voice of God's messengers to you.

➤ Discovery of an Uncommon Moment of Faith…

I once asked a brother if he would like to be healed of his crippled arm. He responded by telling me that doctors had told him his condition was not reversible. When I asked him again if he would like to be healed, he gave the same response, this time including more details about his diagnosis. At this point, I decided to help him; I said, "It's a yes or no answer please; I don't want to hear stories."

He responded by laughing and said I was very funny and had an accent. I walked away thinking of how Jesus could not do many mighty works in His own town. Obviously, this brother did not discover this was an uncommon moment of faith. Great things come in small moments! Only the wise and passionate can discern and unwrap the blessing of the moment.

➢ Discovery of a Divine Harvest…

Many only consider a divine harvest to be financial. They have an incomplete picture. For instance, when I wake up in the morning, I have just received a harvest of a new day from God. When I travel to cities, nations or run errands and come home safely, I have just received another harvest of God's journey mercies and protection. When I eat and drink water without complications, I have just received another harvest from God. We are receiving harvests from God every second of our lives and we should cultivate the attitude of gratitude to God at all times.

It is a blessing to be able to recognize blessings for what they are, Divine Harvests. Many overlook the overflow of God's grace in their lives, by not acknowledging the source of their many gifts. They take for granted many things they have such as their life, health, and ability to speak and walk, not realizing these are part of the harvest. Also, when people are blessed in a manner other than that which they expected, they often fail to recognize God's provision.

➤ Discover your assignment and prosperity will discover you…

When you find and follow your calling in life, your life's purpose—your true assignment—prosperity will find and follow you. Don't just make a living; design a life! Get into the life-work that God designed and engineered YOU for. Live your life by design and you will excel in it.

(6) The Law of Action

Whatever your hand finds to do, do it with all your might.

Ecclesiastes 9:10

…Faith without works is dead…

James 2:26

And whatsoever ye do, do it heartily, as to the Lord, and not unto men.

Colossians 3:23

The above passages show that action is what separates dreamers from achievers! Take daily steps towards your God-inspired dreams and goals. Be committed to what you want to see happen in your life. Get serious enough to put action behind your beliefs. Remember: The road 'someday' leads to the town of nowhere!

(7) The Law of Wisdom

Wisdom is the principal thing. Get wisdom and no matter what it costs, get understanding.

Proverbs 4:7

A wise man will hear and increase in learning.

Proverbs 1:5

Wisdom is knowing and applying Godly principles to solve life's problems and situations. It is the correct application of knowledge. You cannot walk in wisdom without first obtaining knowledge about a subject. You will need personal diligence in order to acquire knowledge.

This means you may have to attend seminars, take training courses, read the right books and upgrade your skills. Make continuous learning and growing a part of your daily routine. Devote time to your personal development. Then you will be able to act in wisdom, applying your knowledge to the situations in your life.

(8) The Law of Relationship & Association

Anyone who walks with the wise will become wise, but the companion of fools will be destroyed.

Proverbs 13:20

Respect the law of association; pursue quality people in your life!

Surround yourself with winners and associate with people who dream big and follow through with action. Choose your friends carefully and only spend time with people who are going to encourage you, lift you higher and challenge you to go to the next level. It is important that you discern and disconnect from toxic relationships. Remember, increase or decrease comes by association.

(9) The Law of Faith

So Jesus answered and said to them, "Have faith in God. ²³For assuredly, I say to you, whoever says to this mountain, 'Be removed and be cast into the sea,' and does not doubt in his heart, but believes that those things he says will be done, he will have whatever he says.

Mark 11:22-23 (NKJV)

Exercise your faith and turn obstacles into opportunities. When facing challenging circumstances, don't get into a mental rut. Refuse to be sidelined or stopped by problems.

The only people without any problems are those in the graveyard! Treat setbacks as temporary hindrances. They are simply stepping stones to becoming the person you need to be, to create the life you want to have. Your faith can move mountains; use it!

(10) **The Law of the Seed**

Honor the LORD with your substance, and with the first fruits of all your increase; [10]so your barns will be filled with plenty, and your vats will overflow with new wine.

Proverbs 3:9-10 (NKJV)

Those who give freely increase all the more and become wealthy; but those who are stingy end up with nothing. [25]The generous man will be prosperous, and he who blesses others will himself be blessed.

Proverbs 11:24-25 (NKJV)

Honor the Lord with your finances and respect the law of sowing and harvest. Be a Tither, Not a Tipper! Be a Sower, Not a Hoarder! Be a Giver, Not a Grabber! The law of the kingdom states: It is more blessed to give than receive! Why? Because as you give more, you get more.

Practicing generosity positions you for a life of ever increasing returns. Bill Gates certainly has lots of critics, but nobody on planet earth can come close to matching his personal giving record of over one billion dollars last year! Yet with all this giving, he continues to be one of the richest men on earth.

His life is proof that a lifestyle of giving sets you up for favor and increase. Utilize these principles. Tithe on the gross, not the net. Giving from your gross, will yield gross blessings.

Giving from the net, will yield net blessings. Give joyfully, gratefully and expectantly! This principle of generosity applies to *all* Christians, believers in business, churches and ministries.

Chapter 11

100 REASONS WHY I HATE POVERTY

(1.) Poverty Is A Tormenting Spirit That Births Agony, Pain And Suffering.

(2.) Poverty Makes You Frown & Instantly Changes Your Countenance From Excitement To A Wrenching Devastation And Heartbreak Whenever There Is A Call To Give…. *Don't Forget It Takes 72 Muscles To Frown & Only 14 To Smile…The More You Frown, The Older You Become!*

(3.) Poverty Is The Climate Where The Seeds Of Suicide Grow And Flourish.

(4.) Poverty Strips People of Their Self-Confidence And Sense Of Self-worth.

(5.) Poverty Is The Number One Vision Killer; It Blurs Dreams And Goals.

(6.) Poverty Breaks The Focus Of Many, Producing Failure.

(7.) Poverty Is Where The Weeds Of Anger And Cynicism Grow The Quickest.

(8.) Poverty Has Never Been And Cannot Be A Friend With Whom To Negotiate.

(9.) Poverty Is A Spiritual & Mental Captivity Which Births Financial Slavery.

(10.) Poverty Literally Stops Missionaries From Planting Churches; Stops Pastors & Evangelists From Embarking On Global Evangelism

(11.) Poverty Is A Spirit That Happens Inside You Before It Happens Outside Of You.

(12.) Poverty Births Fear... Fear Of Failure & Rejection.

(13.) Poverty Is A Plague To Be Stopped.

(14.) Poverty Convinces Many That The Poorer They Are, The Closer They Are To God; What A Lie From The Pit Of Hell!

(15.) Poverty Breaks Marital Relationships.

(16.) Poverty Is A State That Births Domestic Quagmires, Cancerous Nepotism, & Social Stupor Leading To Infrastructural El-dorados.

(17.) Poverty Births Financial Tension And Friction Like A Malicious Dragon.

(18.) Poverty Makes A Country Become A Mere Geographical Expression.

(19.) Poverty Exudes The Offensive Odors Of Oppression & Depression.

(20.) Poverty Constantly Births An Ungodly Fear Of The Unknown.

(21.) Poverty Makes You Live Beneath Your Privilege & Status On The Earth.

(22.) Poverty Is Ugly & Deadly.

(23.) Poverty Makes You Justify Your Lack And Make Excuses Why You Cannot Be A Blessing To Others.

(24.) Poverty Hinders Spontaneous & Swift Obedience To The Voice Of The Holy Spirit And Divine Instructions.

(25.) Poverty Makes You Think That It Is A Crime Or Sin For A Man Or Woman of God To Live In Abundance.

(26.) Poverty Makes You Skeptical & Critical About Sowing Financial Seeds Into The Work of The Lord & Makes The Idea A Mere Impossibility To You.

(27.) Poverty Makes You Hoard & Refuse To Believe That God Is Your Source.

(28.) Poverty Keeps You In A Constant State of Suspicion of Those Around You.

(29.) Poverty Makes You Gluttonous…. *When things are being handed out for free you grab as much as possible, even if you do not need the things.*

(30.) Poverty Feeds Your Disobedience & Rebellion To The Word of God…*Forces You To Rob God By Refusing To Bring The Tithes & Offering To The Lord.*

(31.) Poverty Makes You Believe That Your Financial Source Is The Government, Your Boss, Your Parents, Your Job, or Your Paycheck.

(32.) Poverty Makes You Assume Prosperous Brother or Sisters In Christ Must Be Doing Something Immoral or Illegal.

(33.) Poverty Literally Makes People Forfeit Their Future By Mortgaging It For Peanuts.

(34.) Poverty Strains Relationships; Since We Don't Like People We Owe, it Causes Brothers, Sisters and Best Friends To Become Enemies.

(35.) Poverty Robs & Silences People's Voice & Influence On The Earth.

(36.) Poverty Makes A People Tolerate & Accept Insults & Unpleasant Circumstances.

(37.) Poverty Reduces People To Tears When Faced With A Lawsuit—Not Because They are Guilty, But Because They Lack The Financial Resources To Defend Themselves.

(38.) Poverty Makes You Try Out Many foolish *Get Rich Quick* Schemes, Putting Your Trust In Winning Life-threatening Competitions, or Money Wasting Options Like The Lottery.

(39.) Poverty Makes You Get Angry & Jealous When Others Get Blessed & Share Their Testimonies.

(40.) Poverty Is A Social Stigma Which Births Economic Paralysis & Ethnocentric Chauvinism.

(41.) Poverty Robs You of Your Rest & Makes You Go To Bed Worrying And Having Sleepless Nights About Finances.

(42.) Poverty Constantly Feeds Your Doubt About Your Ability To Become A Financial Pillar.

(43.) Poverty Makes You Console Yourself By Saying If God Wants You Blessed, He Will Bless You!

(44.) Poverty Produces A False Feeling That Others Are Always Disrespecting You.

(45.) Poverty Produces Marital Insecurity Which Leads To Unnecessary Conflicts & Eventually Divorce.

(46.) Poverty Makes You Quit And Give Up Rather Than Succeed In The Journey of Life.

(47.) Poverty Makes You Critical of Those Trying To Set You Free From It.

(48.) Poverty Is A Thief & A Cruel Task Master.

(49.) Poverty Makes You Doubt Every Good Thing About Yourself.

(50.) Poverty Makes You Question The Existence And Love of The Almighty God: Your Source & Provider.

(51.) Poverty Makes You Hate Every Teaching & Teacher of Divine Prosperity.

(52.) Poverty Denies You Access To Quality Health Care For You & Your Family Which May Eventually Lead To Lives Filled With Poor Health and Untimely Deaths.

(53.) Poverty Makes A Man`s Wife Act Like His Mother.

(54.) Poverty Denies You Access To Preferred Nutritious Meals That Will Keep You Healthy.

(55.) Poverty Turns A Courageous Person To A Coward.

(56.) Poverty Destroys Normality; Evil Becomes Good. Right Becomes Wrong.

(57.) Poverty Makes You Draw Unwise Conclusions.

(58.) Poverty Makes You Resentful, Hateful & Ironically Critical of Those Assigned To Bless You, Making You Believe They Must Have Ulterior Motives.

(59.) Poverty Leads To Theft, Aggravated Robbery & Prostitution.

(60.) Poverty Literally Stops Us From Helping Others In Need.

(61.) Poverty Makes Us Doubt The Call And Grace of God On Our Lives.

(62.) Poverty Makes Us Think We Are Always The Subject of Discussion By Others.

(63.) Poverty Makes You Hurry To The Restroom Or Pick Your Bag To Go Home When A Minister Wants To Receive An Offering.

(64.) Poverty Makes Your Heart Skip A Beat Whenever We Hear A Large Amount of Money Is Needed For A Project.

(65.) Poverty Convinces Us That All The Church Talks About Is Money.

(66.) Poverty Convinces You That Sitting At The Feet of A Financial Mentor For An Impartation of Knowledge Is A Waste of Time.

(67.) Poverty Denies You Access To Preferred Quality Education; Answer To So Much Ignorance And Illiteracy.

(68.) Poverty Makes A Man Abandon His Children & Family.

(69.) Poverty Makes Us Borrow From Those We Would Naturally Lend To.

(70.) Poverty Makes You Bow & Say "Yes Sir" To Those That Should Say It To You.

(71.) Poverty Prevents Us From Documenting Our Greatest Persuasions Through The Writing of Books or Through CD Recording Projects.

(72.) Poverty Makes Us Fall Sick Mentally, Psychologically And Physically.

(73.) Poverty Denies Us From Living In Homes, Neighborhoods And Driving Cars of Our Choice.

(74.) Poverty Makes Us Remember And Dwell Only On Past Hurts And Achievements.

(75.) Poverty Makes Sure You Never Become What God Created And Destined You To Be.

(76.) Poverty Causes A Man To Remain A Wisher Rather Than An Accomplished.

(77.) Poverty Births the Continuous Fear That You Will Die In Lack.

(78.) Poverty Eats Up a Person's Ability For Creativity And Productivity.

(79.) Poverty Is A Reproach Which Wears A Garment of Shame and Disgrace.

(80.) Poverty Has A Voice That Says, *"You Can Never Be Debt Free!"*

(81.) Poverty Is Contagious.

(82.) Poverty Robs You of All Resources You Need To Effectively Preach The Gospel.

(83.) Poverty Prolongs And Sometimes Aborts The Fulfillment of Prophecies.

(84.) Poverty Cripples One From Truly and Fully Expressing Their Love, Compassion And Gratitude.

(85.) Poverty Ironically Makes You Live A Lifestyle of Trying To Impress The Joneses by Living Beyond Your Means, Driving You Into More Debt.

(86.) Poverty Is The Spirit That Negatively Reacts The Most In The Presence of A Deliverer, The One Who Can Cast It Out.

(87.) Poverty Limits Your Access To Greatness and Threatens And Challenges Your Confidence To Divine Opportunities.

(88.) Poverty Constantly Kills Your Expectation, the Pleasure God Derives From Your Life.

(89.) Poverty Makes You Believe It's Spiritual To Be Broke.

(90.) Poverty Violently Resents The Laws of God, Which Creates Our Prosperity.

(91.) Poverty Makes You Believe That Financial Captivity Is Natural.

(92.) Poverty Has Not Only Violated God's Perfect Order But It Has Produced A Monumental Fiasco of Great Proportion In Many.

(93.) Poverty Motivates The Killing of Champions From Entering The Earth Through Abortion.

(94.) Poverty Eliminates Your Desired Will In Making Crucial Decisions In Your Life, Family And Marriage.

(95.) Poverty Isolates You, Forcing You To Eat The Bread of Sorrow, Lie On The Bed of Affliction And Sing Songs of Babylon.

(96.) Poverty Causes Constant Nervous Breakdown.

(97.) Poverty Is An Enemy Like Death.

(98.) Poverty Makes You Ignore The Calls of Creditors And Sometimes When You Mistakenly Pick The Call, You Change Your Voice To Act Like You Are Someone Else.

(99.) Poverty Makes Your Life Strange—You Cry When Others Are Laughing And Laugh When Others Are Crying.

(100.) Poverty Is The Last Enemy To Be Conquered Before Jesus Returns.

Chapter 12

THE CONCLUSION

O nce again, there is nothing noble about being poor. Poverty is a part of the curse that came upon mankind after Adam and Eve's disobedience in the Garden of Eden. Ever since this disobedience, man has had to toil in order to be successful. Also, lack has been a reality. However, poverty is not God's will. He desires that we live full, abundant lives, with nothing missing, lacking, or broken.

Jesus came to this earth with a specific purpose - to redeem mankind from everything that fell under the curse. The curse was an empowerment to fail; the curse of sin affected everyone and everything on the earth, including the quality of life that mankind was destined to live. Without Jesus, we would be doomed to a life of failure on earth and an eternity in hell after we die.

Fortunately, Jesus' redemptive work on the cross of Calvary made provision for all who would receive Him as their Lord and Savior.

This means where poverty once reigned, prosperity is now available for everyone who receives it by faith. Separation from God was the inevitable spiritual state of mankind prior to Jesus' death, burial, and resurrection, but through Him we have been brought back into fellowship with the Father. This means we are now His heirs, everything He has belongs to us.

How To Break The Spirit Of Poverty

(1)   Change Your Mindset

For as he thinketh in his heart, so is he...
Proverbs 23:7

Stop thinking your current state is the furthest you will get in life. Think beyond your current job or business; greater things are in store. You can enter your future now in Jesus name!

(2)   Change Your Confession

Confession is the seed for possession. Something you're saying is deciding something God is doing. You will receive and walk in what you say.

Death and life are in the power of the tongue, and those who love it will eat its fruit.
Proverbs 18:21

Stop telling everyone that you are broke. Instead, say this, "Today Is the Poorest I Will Ever Be in Jesus Name!"

(3) Change Your Seed

If you don't like your harvest, then change your seed. Only a lunatic keeps doing the exact same thing, expecting different results. For example, if all your life, you never gave beyond $100.00, change your seed and sow a significant seed of $1000. Name it your Poverty Breaking Seed and expect bigger harvest than you've ever reaped.

> *The LORD God of your fathers make you a thousand times so many more as ye are, and bless you, as he hath promised you!*
> **Deuteronomy 1:11**

(4) Sow Consistently

Some sow once and sit back to watch and see what happens. This is the wrong attitude! Sow consistently. Consistent sowing guarantees consistent reaping. Erratic sowing guarantees erratic reaping.

> *And let us not be weary in well doing: for in due season we shall reap, if we faint not.*
> **Galatians 6:9**

(5) Sow With Expectation of A Harvest

One of the mistakes of my lifetime is not naming seeds I planted. Throughout the Bible, God always encouraged His people to wrap their seed with faith. This is because God blesses our seed in response to our faith. It's not enough to simply give. Give with the expectation of a harvest from your source – Jehovah Jireh, not the person in whom you are sowing.

> *But* **without faith** *it is impossible to please him: for he that cometh to God must believe that he is, and that he is a rewarder of them that diligently seek him.*

Hebrews 11:6

(6) Following Divine Instructions

An Instruction is an opportunity to prove your competence. God promises a floodgate of blessings if we would just follow His instructions.

> *If thou shalt hearken diligently unto the voice of the LORD thy God, to observe and to do all his commandments which I command thee this day…...*
> *The LORD shall open unto thee his good treasure, the heaven to give the rain unto thy land in his season, and to bless all the work of thine hand……..*

Deuteronomy 28: 1-14

Say To Yourself, "I am a receiver of everything God has for me!" Financial success is closer to you than you think. I don't care how much debt you have.

I don't care if you think you don't make enough money. I don't care about your education. I don't even care about your family history.

None of that can stop your financial success. Ask God for financial blessings then start sowing consistently, expecting God to produce an abundant harvest and proclaiming to all who will hear that your harvest is coming. Your reward is already on its way!

More Scriptures about Finances

In all labour there is profit, but idle talk leads only to poverty.
Proverbs 14:23 (Amplified)

Steady plodding brings prosperity; hasty speculation brings poverty.
Proverbs 21:5 (NIV)

He that tilleth his land shall have plenty of bread: but he that followeth after vain persons shall have poverty enough.
Proverbs 28:19 (KJV)

For ye have the poor with you always, and whensoever ye will ye may do them good: but me ye have not always.

Mark 14:7 (KJV)

Being enriched in everything to all bountifulness, which causeth through us thanksgiving to God.

2 Corinthians 9:11 (KJV)

And God is able to make all grace (every favor and earthly blessing) come to me in abundance, so that I may always and under all circumstances and whatever the need, be self-sufficient — possessing enough to require no aid or support and furnished in abundance for every good work and charitable donation."
2 Corinthians 9:8 (Amplified)

And you will be called priests of the LORD, you will be named ministers of our God. You will feed on the wealth of nations, and in their riches you will boast. ⁷Instead of their shame my people will receive a double portion.
Isaiah 61:6-7

Fear the LORD; you his saints, for those who fear him lack nothing.
Psalm 34:9

*This is what the LORD says, … **I will give them all the prosperity I have promised them.***
Jeremiah 32:42 (NIV)

I restore your fortunes before your very eyes," says the LORD.
Zephaniah 3:20 (NIV)

A sinner's wealth is stored up for the righteous.
Proverbs. 13:22 (NIV)

Blessed is the man who fears the Lord; wealth and riches will be in his house.
Psalm 112:1,3 (NKJV)

As for the rich in this world, charge them not to be proud and arrogant and contemptuous of others, nor to set their hopes on uncertain riches, but on God, Who richly and ceaselessly provides us with everything for [our] enjoyment.

1 Timothy 6:17 (Amplified)

Quotes From Remarkable Achievers

Remember the poor - it costs nothing.
(Mark Twain)

The most terrible poverty is loneliness and the feeling of being unloved.
(Mother Teresa)

The mother of revolution and crime is poverty.
(Aristotle)

Poverty often deprives a man of all spirit and virtue; it is hard for an empty bag to stand upright.
(Benjamin Franklin)

Notes & Reflections

Salvation Call

Now the choice is yours. Will you accept the Lord Jesus Christ as your Personal Lord and Savior?

If we confess our sins, he is faithful and just to forgive us our sins and to cleanse us from all unrighteousness.

(1 John 1:9)

Dear Lord Jesus, I come to you just as I am. I am a sinner. I need forgiveness. I am sorry for my sins. I believe You died on the cross for MY sins. I also believe that you rose from the dead, ascended into heaven and coming back again for me. Please forgive me, wash and cleanse me with your precious blood. Purge my conscience from dead works. Come into my heart and give me a new life. Thank You, Jesus, for shedding your blood for me and for hearing and answering my prayer. I receive grace to live for you. Thank You Father for accepting me today, I am Born Again and Heaven Is my home In Jesus` Name, Amen!

Luke 15:10 says;

Likewise, I say unto you, there is joy in the presence of the angels of God over one sinner that repenteth.

Yes…Bro. Courage, I made a decision to accept the Lord Jesus Christ today as my Lord and Personal Savior and I would like to receive materials that would help me in my walk with God.

Name ....

Address ....

City ....

State .... Zip ....

Phone ....

Email: pastorcourage@jgmsite.org
Website: www.jgmsite.org

ABOUT THE AUTHOR

From the age of twelve, Courage Igene has preached the undiluted gospel of Jesus Christ with signs & wonders and miracles following. Untold thousands have been saved and set free around the world through God using him remarkably in the Sign-Gift ministry.

He is the founder and president of Joshua Generation Ministries (JGM) which involves:

- Church Planting (All Nations House of Worship)
- JGM School of Ministry (Ministry Training)
- Nationwide Healing Rain Crusades
- Live Prophetic Telephone Prayer Conferences.

An accomplished author, Courage Igene has written other thought provoking, insightful and anointed books, namely: God's Weapons of Mass Destruction, Revelation & Relationship.

His passion for worship has been described by many as the secret to the tangible healing & prophetic anointing on his life. His joy, love for God and people is contagious. He may be coming to a city near you. You will love his ministry! And as he always say: "We shall see what we shall see in Jesus name!"

OTHER BOOKS BY THE MINISTRY

God's Weapons of Mass Destruction brings answers to your questions on spiritual warfare. The difference between yesterday and your tomorrow is knowledge. What you do not know is capable of harming you. As a good soldier of the cross, whose commander-in-chief is the Lord Jesus Christ, this book enlightens you on the weapons available to you. They command Heaven's attention, earth's reaction and hell's destruction. As long as a Child of God lives, attacks are inevitable. Many have said to me; "Bro. Courage, why am I under so much attack?" Someone suggested; "But I am a good person.

I try to please everyone." I respond by giving them this scripture; "They compassed me about also with words of hatred; and fought against me without a cause." (Psalm 109:3) Job came under attack because he was an upright man who loved the Lord and hated evil. (Job 1:1) Now more than ever, he unleashes his rage and destruction against people because he knows that his time is short. Christians especially experience strange attacks, both physical and spiritual, day and night. In such conditions, we are not expected to be helpless or defenseless, rather, we are supposed to be equipped with God's Weapons of Mass Destruction to sustain our victory against our arch-enemy who is Satan the devil and his cohorts.

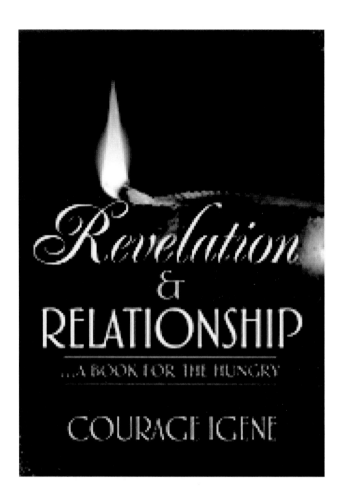

The difference between your past and your future is your knowledge. Someone knows something you don't know. Never be afraid of the devil but be afraid of ignorance. It's the only reason people walk in error and perish (Hosea 4:6). This book is for the hungry and those who are sincerely tired of the harassment of the enemy.

In This Book, You Learn:

- ➤ 20 ways to identify someone with a religious spirit
- ➤ The power of extreme obedience
- ➤ The missing ingredient
- ➤ Father, Son, Holy Spirit…3 Gods or 1?
- ➤ Who is this Jesus?
- …and much more!

All your spoken and unspoken questions about the true deity of The Lord Jesus Christ are answered in this book without compromise. This Revelation cut across religious dogmas and traditional systems.

Revelation & Relationship:

A Manual for Truth, Spiritual Transformation and Divine Encounter!

You can order these priceless books @

www.jgmsite.org
www.amazon.com
www.barnesandnoble.com